OPENING THE ELLEN FILES

HILLTOP PRESS

ACKNOWLEDGEMENTS

The ballad texts reprinted here are versions included by Robert Jamieson in his collection 'Popular Ballads and Songs of Tradition, Manuscript, and Scarce Editions' (A. Constable, Edinburgh, 1806)

British Library Cataloguing in Publication Data

A catalogue record for this book is available from the British Library

ISBN 0 905262 33 6

Hilltop Press titles are distributed overseas by BBR/NSFA
www.bbr-online.com/catalogue

Hilltop Press
4 Nowell Place, Almondbury, Huddersfield,
West Yorkshire, HD5 8PB,
England.

(Price £1.75 / $4.00

(Cheques/POs/Checks payable to S. Sneyd, not to the Press by name.)

INTRODUCTION

In the early 1800, Robert Jamieson, a Scot teaching in Macclesfield and passing some lonely spare time translating some old Danish ballads, noticed some curious resemblances between the one such's story and a tale he'd heard as a boy from a packman.

Both told of a girl, in each case an Ellen, stolen away by an Otherish being. Jamieson, at the time, was also busily compiling a massive collection of Scottish ballads. He became convinced that amongst them he had found the sequel to this episode. Widely-distributed, in many variants, it told of the ordeals of a girl, again usually Helen or Ellen, at the hands of an uncaring impregnator. Whether pregnant, usually near term, or already having his child (or in some cases children to the magic number of seven) she is set humiliating tests - to undertake a physically taxing journey, sometimes involving the passage of a dangerous river, to go in male disguise as an inferior servant, even to serve the cruel lover's new wife. Only thus can she achieve acceptance and recognition for herself and her child at his family dwelling or stronghold. This, thought Jamieson, completed a fragmented Ellen epic.

The story he recalled from his Morayshire childhood (it and the Danish ballad are both too long to reprint here, hence these brief summaries), a c(h)antefable or mix of prose and verse telling, begins with three brothers and a sister, children of King Arthur and Queen Ginevra (sic), playing football. The ball is kicked over a church. The young sister Burd (an unmarried girl) Ellen goes to fetch it and doesn't come back. In turn, the two older boys go in search. Neither returns. Then it is the turn of the third, Childe (an adolescent not yet knightable) Rowland; killing all he meets along the way to prevent forewarning of his coming, he reaches the Elf King's barrow mound castle to find his brothers dead and Ellen imprisoned. Rowland defeats the King, forces him to resurrect the brothers, and all go safe home. (Jamieson also believed this lay behind Edgar's 'King Lear' line "Childe Roland to the dark tower came", later Browning's inspiration.)

In the Danish ballad, from the Kaempe Viser of 1591, Rosmer Hafmand, a sea-giant, steals away Ellen-lille to his island. When her brother Roland arrives in search of her, she persuades the giant to spare him and let him stay. After two years, pregnant by Roland, she fears the giant's wrath. Roland persuades Rosmer to carry him back to the mainland, tricking him into bringing along the kist (treasure chest) in which Ellen has hidden so that she too safely escapes, though with the burden of incestuous pregnancy to explain on her return.

(Since Arthur's nemesis, Mordred, was born of the hero-king's incest with his half-sister, it is intriguing that "Child Rowland" repeats in the next generation a pattern that may reflect a similar tactical response to matrilineal inheritance rules, in Pictish Scotland, to that of the ruling families of Pharaonic and Ptolemaic Eygpt.)

The ballads and extracts on the following pages variously illustrate Ellen's subsequent ordeals. As with so much folkmaterial, realistic and fantasy elements overlap as on a Venn diagram. or as the Elven Other world enters ours. Her enforced stress-filled journey could aim to solve the problem by inducing miscarriage, yet it also parallels the dark magic of these routes, to the Otherworld, or death itself, along which demon lovers lure their prey. Other ordeals appear aimed to induce the humiliated Ellen to respond by infanticide, as overstressed animals kill their young, yet also hint at the shapechangings that insert fairy changelings into human households. The curious episode of the Billy Blin can be read as a spiteful witch trying to prevent the arrival of an embarassing or threatening grandchild; yet also the birth's impossible delay recalls how differently time runs in Faerie, as, in Einsteinian theory, it will for near-light-speed startravellers. Jamieson's posited rediscovery of a fragmented epic may or may not hold water, nor have we here that wondrous Helen, Troy's, Faustus sold his soul to know; yet we do indeed darkly glimpse some of fantasy's deepest, most abiding,roots.

SOURCES: Popular Ballads and Songs from Tradition, Manuscript, and Scarce Editions, by Robert Janieson, John Constable, Edinburgh, 1806; Illustrations of Northern Antiquities, from the Earlier Teutonic and Scandinavian Romances. by H.W. Weber, R Jamieson, & WS (Walter Scott), John Ballantyne & Co., Edinburgh, 1814.

BURD ELLEN

Lord Thomas stands by his stable-door,
    Seeing his steed kaim'd down;
Lady Ellen sits at her bower door,
    Sewing her silver seam.

"O will ye stay at hame, Ellen,
    And sew your silver seam?
Or will ye to the rank highlands,
    For my lands lay far frae hame?"

"I winna stay at hame, Lord Thomas,
    And sew my silver seam;
Buit I will gae to the rank highlands,
    Tho' your lands lay far frae hame."

* * * * *

"An asking, an asking, lord Thomas;
    I pray thee grant it me:
How many miles into your fair tower,
    And house where you would be?"

"Your asking fair, lady Ellen," he says,
    "Shall now be granted thee;
For to my castle where it stands,
    Is thirty miles and three."
"O wae is me," says lady Ellen,
    "It will never be run by me."

But up and spak the wily pyot,
    That sat upon the tree,
"Sae loud, sae loud, ye fause fause knight,
    Sae loud as I hear ye lie;

"For to your dwelling-house," it says,
    "Of miles it's scantly three."
"O weel is me," Says lady Ellen,
    It shall be run by me."

"O mither, mither, mak my bed,
    And mak it braid and wide;
And lay my little page at my feet,
    Whatever may betide."

* * * * *

"An asking, an asking, lord Thomas,
    I pray thee, grant it me:
O grant me a cup of cold water
    Between my young son and me."

"What you do ask, lady Ellen,
    Shall soon be granted thee;
The best bread, and the best wine,
    Between my young son and thee."

"I ask again, my good lord Thomas,
    I ask again of thee,
The poorest cot-house in your land
    Between my young son and me."

"Your asking, now, dear lady Ellen,
    I quickly grant to thee;
The best bower about my tower,
    Between my young son and thee."

* * * * *

BURD ELLEN

A Journey extracted from another version

LORD JOHN stood in his stable door,
    Said he was boun to ride;
Burd Ellen stood in her bower door,
    Said she'd rin by his side.

He's pitten on his cork-heeled shoon,
    And fast awa rade he;
She's clad hersel in page array,
    And after him ran she,

Till they came till a wan water,
    And folks do call it Clyde;
Then he's lookit o'er his left shoulder,
    Say's "Lady, will ye ride?"

"O, I learnt it wi' my bower woman,
    And I learnt it from my weal,
Whanever I cam to wan water,
    To swim like ony eel."

But the firsten stap the lady stappit,
The water came till her knee;
"Ochon, alas!" said the lady,
"This water's o'er deep for me."

The nexten stap the lady stappit,
The water came till her middle;
And, sighing, says that gay lady,
"I've wet my gouden girdle."

The thirden stap the lady stappit,
The water came till her pap;
And the bairn that was in her twa sides
For cauld began to quake.

"Lie still, lie still, my ain dear babe;
Ye work your mother wae,
Your father rides on high horseback,
Cares little for us twae."

O, about the midst o' Clyde's water
There was a yeard-fast stane;
He lightly turned his horse about,
And took her on him behin.

"O, tell me this now, good Lord John,
And a word ye dinna lie,
How far is it to your lodgin,
Whare we this night maun be?"

"O see na ye yon castell, Ellen,
That shines sae fair to see?
There is a lady in it, Ellen,
Will sinder you and me."

BURD HELEN

From the recitation of Mrs Arrot

There liv'd a lord on yon sea-side,
And he thought on a wile,
How he would go over the saut sea
A lady to beguile.

"O learn to mak your bed, Helen,
And learn to ly your lane;
For I'm gaun over the saut seas
A bright bride to bring hame."

"How can I mak my bed," she says,
"Unless I mak it wide,
Whan I have seven o' your sons
To lie down by my side?

"And the first o' your seven sons,
He rides a milk-white steed;
The second o' your seven sons
He wears a milk-white weed;

"The third ane o' your seven sons,
He draws baith ale and wine;
The fourth ane o' your seven sons,
He serves you when you dine;

"The fifth ane o' your seven sons,
He can baith read and write;
The sixth ane o' your seven sons,
He is a' your heart's delight;

"And the youngest o' your seven sons,
He sleeps on my breast-bane;
Whan him and I ly down at night,
From him rest get I nane."

"O wha will bake my bridal bread,
And brew my bridal ale?
And wha will welcome my gae lady
That I bring o'er the dale?

"And sin ye've ta'en the turn in hand,
    See that ye do it right,
And ilka chimly o' the house,
    That they be dearly dight."

O a' the day she wash'd and wrang,
    And a' the night she buik,
And she's awa' to her chamber
    To gie her young son suck.

"Come here, come here, my eldest son,
    And see what ye may see;
For yonder comes your father dear,
    Your mother-in-law side be."

She's ta'en a cake o' the best bread,
    A bottle o' the best wine,
And a' the keys upon her arm,
    And to the yates she's gaen.

"Ye are welcome hame, gay lady," she said,
    "And ay ye are welcome hame;
And sae is a' the gentlewomen
    That's wi' you ridden and gane.

"You are welcome hame, gay lord," she said,
    "And ay ye are welcome hame;
And sae is a' the gentlemen
    That's wi' you ridden and gane."

She sair'd them up, she sair'd them down,
    She sair'd them till and frae;
But then she went behind their backs,
    The tear did blind her e'e.

Whan day was gane and night was come,
    And a' man boun' to bed,
The bridegroom and the bonny bride
    In their chamber was laid.

Burd Helen and her seven sons
    Lay in a bower nearby;
★ ★ ★ ★ ★ ★
    ★ ★ ★ ★ ★ ★

"If my seven sons were seven grey ratts,
    To rin frae wa' to wa',
And I mysel' a good grey cat,
I would bite their back a-twa.

"If my seven sons were seven grey hares,
    And them to rin a race,
And I mysel' a good greyhound,
    I would gi'e them a chace."

Up and spak the bonny bride
    In chamber where she lay, —
"There is lady in this bower,
    She will gae mad or day."

"Lye still, lye still, my bonny bride,
    Lye still and tak a sleep;
Its but ane o' my wine puncheons;
    Nae longer wad it keep."

"King Henry was my father dear,
    Queen Catharine was my mother,
Lady Anne she was my sister dear,
    And Frederick was my brother.

"And whan I was six years of age,
    They ca'd me *Mary Mild:*
I was stown frae my father's yate,
    Whan I was but a child."

The up and spak the bonny bride,
    By her lord as she lay, —
"Lye down, lye down, my dear sister,
    There's nae ill done for me.

"O seven ships convey'd me here,
    And seven came o'er the main;
And four o' them shall stay wi' you,
    And three convey me hame.

"But when I gae hame to my father's house,
    They will laugh me to scorn,
To come awa' a wedded wife,
    Gae hame a maid the morn."

THE BILLY BLIN

And ay at ilka silver hem
Hings fifty silver bells and ten;
That goodly gift shall be your ain,
And let her be lighter o' her young bairn."

"O' her young bairn she's never be lighter,
Nor in her bower to shine the brighter;
But she shall die and turn to clay,
And you shall wed anither may."
"Anither may I'll never wed,
Anither may I'll never bring hame;"
But, sighing, says that weary wight,
"I wish my days were at an en'!"

He did him till his mither again,
That vile rank witch o' vilest kin,
And said, "My lady has a steed,
The likes o' him's nae i' the lands o' Leed;
For he is gouden shod before,
And he is gouden shod behin';
And at ilka tate o' that horse' mane
There's a gouden chess and bell ringin';

"This goodly gift sall be your ain,
and lat her be lighter o' her young bairn."
"O' her young bairn she's never be lighter,
Nor in her bower to shine the brighter,
But she shall die and go to clay,
And you shall wed anither may."

"Another may I'll never wed,
Anither may I'll never bring hame;"
But, sighing, says that weary wight,
"I wish my life were at an en'!"
Then out it spak the Billy Blin,
He spak ay in a good time,
"Ye do you to the market-place,
And there ye buy a leaf o' wax.

"Ye shape it bairn and bairnly like,
And in twa glazen een ye pit;
And do you to your mither then
And bid her to your boy's Christnin',
For dear's the boy he's been to you;
Then notice well what she shall do;
And do you stand a little forbye,
And listen well what she will say."

He did him to the market-place,
And there he bought a leaf o' wax;
He shaped it bairn and bairnly like,
And in twa glazen een he pat;

He did him to his mither then,
And bade her to his boy's Christnin';
And he did stand a little forbye
And noticed well what she did say.

"O wha has loos'd the nine witch knots,
That was amang that lady's locks?
And wha's ta'en out the kaimbs o' care,
That was amang that lady's hair?
And wha has kill'd the master kid,
That ran aneath that lady's bed?
And wha has loos'd her left-foot shee,
And latten that lady lighter be?"

"O Willy has loos'd the nine witch knots
That hang amang the lady's locks;
And Willy's a'en out the kaimbs o' care,
That hang amang his lady's hair;
And Willy's killed the master kid,
That ran aneath his lady's bed;
And Willy's loos'd her left-foot shee,
And latten his lady lighter be.

It damned near killed me.
You are massive. What I have always
Wanted to ride with the wind.
That wild look in your eyes.
Could it be you or is this
Just some mad girl's fancy?
Only one young man in the village
Saw beyond the stumble and the limp.
Always gave me the same smile
Whether I impressed or not in my
Uneven way. We had no chance.
His parents wouldn't countenance it.
The sun must shine. God must be happy in His heaven
And legs must be even.
I pull the reins and lead you to the gate.
It is my ladder to the stars.
This is a game. I can't believe my daring.
I lie across your back and neck
Taut equine musky musculature.
Ride my black beauty ride.
We are away. You seem to know
Exactly where to go. I have no fear
Of falling.
Crossing the ford was easy.
Plashes scattering the ghosts of night.
Marsh gas rising from the hollow
Like a sepulchral cloak.
The reeds rustling while fox cubs play.
Moonbeams dancing as we gather speed.
Hooves hammering tattoos in the turf.
The world passes in a cold draft.
And my body thrums with your beat.
A bit like being excited after a dance
Only you are doing it.
We run and twist and leap through space.
The air is just a journey like the ground.
Broken rhythm: sound, silence, sound.
And we are nearly there, you slow, my parents' house.
I hang, slide down your sweaty flank,
Approach the door. My mother opens it.
She gapes, stares past me in amazement.
No dark horse, just a man
His feet and hands all bloody.
She seems to understand no explanations are required.
We bathe his hands and feet.
He falls into a sleep.
And as the firelight flickers in the grate
I stroke your long black hair
Without regret, as a lover might.

A DARK HORSE FANTASY

Nightmare! What - someone in the room.
Don't move. Don't scream.
Why must I always sleep alone.
I'm not that quick. My heart
Can't keep up with itself.
The thumping chamber springs my breath
At last I gasp but nothing moves.
The thief has gone. Was it all dream shadows?
I look inside but it's not the pain
Or it's remembered fever
Dared not rob me of my sleep tonight.
I'm too hard worked yet I feel robbed
As if I have lost something more than fate allowed.
As if I have been touched against my will.
My father was afraid, discharged his duty
And sent me to the castle to tender as a scullery maid.
The work is hard and I am getting used to going
Without the light. But I don't like it.
The butler and the cook give me the evil eye
It's not my fault that I'm a hopalong.
I would have been a beautiful girl
A really beautiful one. I have the bosom
And the hair - lovely long red hair.
Oh! No this is a nightmare - this
Has to be a dream. Wake up! Wake up!
They cut my hair off while I slept.
Those bastards.
The world would leave you with no dignity at all.
So I will leave this undignified world.
I dress and waddle down the draughty stairs.
Voices in the kitchen cough like phlegm.
It is them.
- By this red hair we bind the demon in
- Our midst. Return ye to the fires of hell
- As this hair is consumed by fire.
I can't believe this. Bad enough to live with
This pain from my leg but heart
Pains are not so easily endured.
Deformity sure makes the seeing blind
And their deformed hopalong hearts
Lurch when it comes to love.
I will not be ashamed.
Amazing how desperation makes us brave.
I am heading for the stables. It has been
Six years since I last rode a horse.

ABOUT THE AUTHOR

Jimmie Dickie was born in Irvine, Ayshire, Scotland, in 1962. Now living in Aberdeen, and working as an accountant, he says "Some knights-move thinking might be required to understand my "career", which has lurched from psychiatric nursing to physiology to accounting.

Of his writing, he says "my earliest heroes were Dan Dare, Rupert Bear, and Doctor Who. By the age of twelve I was under the spell of Asimov, Clarke, Ballard, and Aldiss, Philip Jose Farmer and Michael Moorcock."

The Poem printed here, however, draws its inspiration not so much from the imaginings of such science fiction giants, but from a much older source, those traditional folk tales and ballads of his native country, which so inseparably entwine the lives of our world with the invasive strangness of the realm of the Other.

COPYRIGHT & ACKNOWLEDGEMENTS

The poem was previously published on the House of Moonlight website.

British Library Cataloguing in Publication Date
A catalogue record for this book is available from the British Library

ISBN 0 905262 33 6

Hilltop Press titles are distributed overseas by BBR/NSFA
www.bbr-online.com/catalogue

HILLTOP PRESS
4 Nowell Place, Almondbury, Huddersfield,
West Yorkshire, HD5 8PB, England.

Price £1.75 / $4.00

(Cheques/POs/checks payable to S. Sneyd, not to the Press by name)

A DARK HORSE FANTASY

by

JIMMIE DICKIE

Hilltop Press